Acknowledgn

Vatican Documents - V.I.S. - Vatican Information S

Excerpt from Educating for Life by Thomas Gr‿   ‿ ‿nomas More an
imprint of Ave Maria Press, P.O. Box 428, Notre Dame, Indiana, 46556. Used with
permission of the publisher. www.avemariapress.com

Extract taken from Free to Believe by Michael Paul Gallagher SJ, published and
copyright 1987 by Darton, Longman and Todd Ltd, and used by permission of
publisher

*We have made every effort to contact copyright holders and seek their permission to
use their material. If any involuntary infringement of copyright has occurred, we offer
our apologies and will correct any error in future editions.*

ISBN 0-9544539-6-4

Don Bosco Publications
Thornleigh House
Bolton BL1 6PQ
Tel 01204 308 811

DEDICATION

**In the spirit of St John Bosco, patron of the young,
these reflections are dedicated:**

To our young people created in the image and likeness of God who live in a great variety of situations, some loving and enriching, some less loving and impoverishing.

To those who take up the mission and challenge of walking the journey of life and faith with young people, acknowledging and addressing their questions, needs, concerns, hopes and aspirations.

To those who take up this mission in a variety of roles in the context of our Catholic Schools: an educating community inspired by the Christian faith vision.

We are called to the same mission and are aware of its supreme importance: young people are at the age when they must make basic life-choices which affect the future of society and the Church.
                                        Salesian Constitution no 26

In general it is the young who are the first victims of the spiritual and cultural crisis gripping the world. It is also true that any commitment to the betterment of society finds its hopes in them. This should stimulate the Church all the more to proclaim the Gospel to the world of youth with courage and creativity.
                                    General Directory for Catechesis no 181

CONTENTS

WHY THESE REFLECTIONS?

At the end of in-service days, a number of those present frequently ask for copies of some of my overheads which normally contain some key quotations. Those who make the request say that they would like more time to reflect on them personally or be able to use them in their schools, either as part of the daily or weekly briefings or in staff reflection and discussion. These reflections are, in a sense, a response to those requests. I include some of the key quotations which I use on these occasions. I have added others that I see as significant, I do not usually present them because of the limitation of time, or because they are not always appropriate for a particular group.

I have focussed on aspects of the religious dimension of education in a Catholic School: an educating community inspired by Christian faith and beliefs about people, life and the world. My main sources are the directives and guidance set out in Church documents, and other writings which deal with key features of Catholic Schooling. I also draw on my own experience over the years in a variety of roles within Catholic education.

Headteachers, members of the management team and others are well versed in, or at least well aware of, the vast number of documents that come from the government. Church texts on the nature and purpose, as well as key features, of the education offered in a Catholic School are less well known. Often, even when known, many find them difficult to read, especially when they seem to be written in theological or philosophical language. It is not always easy to set aside time for such reading and reflection in the busy schedule of our schools. Yet it would seem essential that those who devote themselves to education in Catholic Schools, particularly those who seek to take up leadership roles in them, should be acquainted with these directives, guidance and ideas.

Recently one Governor expressed surprise at the relevance of what is stated in these documents. Till then she was unaware of them. There are many hidden treasures in these texts and writings. They can, and do inspire and challenge us, to explore in greater depth the nature and purpose of education in a Catholic School. They may help us to re-examine some distinctive features of the education which we should seek to provide in our schools. This is particularly necessary in these times of constant and rapid developments and changes in society, the Church and educational policy.

I present in these pages a number of key quotations from Church documents and other writings which have made an impression on me and have appealed to teachers and others. Some quotations are longer than I would normally present at in-service courses. However, I feel it would be useful to have the opportunity to read and reflect on them. It is unlikely that many will have the opportunity to read the whole of the documents, unless they are doing a dissertation on Catholic Schooling. What I present here are some reflections of a pastoral and theological nature, not an in-depth study of Catholic Schooling. I do not explore in any specific way the value and importance of classroom Religious Education.

The quotations and reflections will certainly not provide immediate and practical solutions to the many complex problems and issues which face school staffs and Governors, in the daily round of running our schools. As the Church document on The Catholic School states, *they do not provide a quick answer to contemporary problems, but they give a direction which can begin to solve them.*[1] These reflections are offered as a word of hope and encouragement to all those involved in our schools at the beginning of the 21st century, a daunting, demanding and exciting time.

---

[1] *The Catholic School* no 67

PAUSE, REFLECT, AFFIRM

Teaching has an extraordinary moral depth and is one of the most excellent and creative human activities, for the teacher does not write on inanimate material, but on the very spirits of human beings. The personal relationships between teacher and the students, therefore, assume an enormous importance and are not limited to giving and taking.

The Catholic School on the Threshold of the Third Millennium no 19

The school must be a community whose values are communicated through the interpersonal and sincere relationships of its members and through both individual and corporate adherence to the outlook on life that permeates the school.

The Catholic School no 32

It must never be forgotten that the school is always in the process of being created, due to the labour brought to fruition by all who have a role to play in it, and most especially by those who are teachers.

Lay Catholics in School no 78

Over the years I have visited many schools, addressed many school staffs and Governors and I have facilitated conferences of Headteachers, Deputy Heads, Heads of Religious Education and others. I am constantly moved to find so many teachers affected by what I term the three D-verbs: discouraged, demoralised but dedicated. I am deeply conscious of how pressurised and harassed many teachers feel when faced with a constant stream of government initiatives, with preparing, marking, and testing, increased paper work and with many other demands on their time and energy. They can feel at times that they are little appreciated by many outside the profession, too readily blamed, not so frequently praised. Yet however tired and weary, there is still among most teachers a love for the task, for the mission with children and the young and for the service they provide for them, their families, for society and the Church.

Making Time and Space

It is for this reason that it is good occasionally to set aside a day or part of a day to reflect together and reaffirm the true worth of the task, despite the difficulties, concerns and problems. By creating the space and time for such reflection and sharing, we can be better prepared to accept and face the difficulties which are part and parcel of any vocation. These difficulties need not cloud the vision of what is truly valuable and of great worth in the task of serving the young of the 21st century in our schools.

In-service days are not always popular. Some may be reluctant to deal with what they consider the less practical aspect of education such as reflecting on Catholic ethos. This can seem to be concerned with abstract idealism or to be the particular task of the RE staff, chaplains, pastoral staff or senior management. This area of the religious dimension of education in Catholic Schools is the theme of my reflections. Despite some initial reluctance, most staff express their appreciation of having dedicated time and space for such reflection and sharing.

Generally, staff have felt inspired, challenged and affirmed in the work they do individually and corporately. Although what is said in talks and discussions is for the most part a remarkable grasp of the obvious, in the daily rush of school life there is little time to see and affirm the obvious. We need to recognise the good work that is being done by individual members of staff in their specific roles and by the whole staff, working as a team, to address the great variety of needs and capabilities of the pupils. They invariably feel affirmed and to some extent challenged.

Working Together

Every school has its mission statement which seeks to express the core of its vision of sound education and the spirit which should permeate every aspect of the life of the school. In a Catholic School this will be expressed in the light of our Christian belief in the dignity, worth and uniqueness of each individual person. In a Catholic School we believe in the importance and centrality of a healthy, caring community for true personal development. Underpinning and motivating such expressions of our mission is not just educational theory, there is also a Christian theology of Creation, Incarnation and Trinity.

In our schools not all pupils and members of staff are Catholic. In large secondary schools as many as half the staff may be of other Christian denominations, of other faiths or may claim to be of none, while upholding certain basic human values. Although all members of staff are not of the same community of faith, on taking up their post, they become members of an educating community whose inspiration and motivation for the work of education is founded in the Christian faith and Gospel. This is spelt out in the Mission Statement and other school policy statements. When all staff adhere to such a vision and seek to make it a reality in the daily life in the school, then such diversity can be enriching and should be employed wisely to build up the educating community of the school in our multi-cultural and multi-faith society. In this way we can ensure that our schools achieve what the bishops have recently stated:

The quality of what is offered in our institutions is, almost without exception, highly regarded and commented upon favourably in official inspections. Far from being a divisive influence, all available evidence points to denominational education making a significant contribution in preparing young people to take a proper place in the diverse society in which we live.[2]

On in-service days I suggest that some time during the day or afterwards each member of staff should approach another member of staff and say, "Thanks for what you do. It is not something I can do but I appreciate the fact that you do it." Individually we cannot serve all the needs of all pupils - academic, physical, social, cultural, emotional, spiritual and religious. As a team, with common vision and aims, we can try. Let's appreciate and thank each other. Let's create some dedicated space and time to do so.

*It takes a whole village
to educate a child.*

Chinese Proverb

---

[2] Bishops' Statement *Catholic Schools Serving Our Society*

Pause for Reflection

In the busy routine of daily life in school can I and do I find time and space to reflect on the value and worth of my work?

Can I find such time and space at other times?

As a staff, do we set aside time for reflection on, and affirmation of, what we seek to do together for the pupils, their families and all members of staff?

Is it important to do so?

How can this be done?

EDUCATION - A CONSTANT FEATURE
OF THE CATHOLIC TRADITION

When one considers the influence of Catholic Christianity on Western education and civilisation and adds in its missionary work throughout the world, it does not seem an exaggeration to claim that no single agency in human history has educated more people than Catholicism – and has done so in a life-giving way. Although undoubtedly falling short at times of its own ideals, nevertheless, Catholic education can claim a rich legacy.

Tom Groome: Educating for Life p 48

At great cost and sacrifice our forbears were inspired by the teaching of the Church to establish schools which enrich mankind and responded to the needs of time and place. While it recognises its own inadequacies, the Catholic School is conscious of its responsibility to continue this service.

The Catholic School no 65

A Mission through the Centuries

The Catholic Church has been involved in the mission of education down through the centuries. Today its involvement in education of the human person is worldwide.

The bishops at Vatican II made a declaration that spells out the importance given by the Church to the work of education, not only at that particular moment in history, but as a constant feature of the Church's mission.

All people of whatever race, condition or age, in virtue of their dignity as human persons, have an inalienable right to education. This education should be suitable to the particular destiny of the individuals, adapted to their ability, sex and national cultural traditions, and should be conducive to amicable relations with other nations in order to promote true unity and peace in the world. True education aims to give people a formation which is directed towards their final end and the good of the society to which they belong and in which, as adults, they will have their share of duties to perform.[3]

Historically, we need only recall the schools attached to the monasteries and the cathedrals. Later there came the great universities, Salerno, Bologna, Paris, Oxford, Cambridge and others. These were an important feature of the Church's mission to education, the degrees were granted by papal charter and the professors were, for the most part, clergy, e.g. Dominicans, Franciscans, Augustinians. Many religious congregations, both male and female, were founded precisely for the mission of education, in many cases for the poor and disadvantaged who had no access to the education provided by others. In many countries, Catholic parishes built schools often with the pennies of the poor.

---

[3] Vatican II *Declaration on Christian Education* no 1

A Worldwide Mission

Wherever Catholic missionaries go they set up schools. Today Catholic Schools can be found in most countries of the world, including those in which Catholics are a minority. In many of these schools a large number of pupils are not Catholic and do not choose to become Catholic, for example in a number of Asian and African countries. A recent Church document speaks of a dimension of openness in such situations and goes on to say that in such countries *Catholic Schools have always promoted civil progress and human development without discrimination of any kind.*[4] This reiterates what was said in the document *The Catholic School*:

> *In the certainty that the Spirit is at work in every person, the Catholic School offers itself to all, including non-Christians, with all its distinctive aims and means, acknowledging, preserving and promoting the spiritual and moral qualities, social and cultural values, which characterise different civilisations.*[5]

Many of my fellow Salesians in India, Tunisia and elsewhere run schools in which few pupils are Christians and in which proselytising and seeking converts is not encouraged or absolutely forbidden under threat of imprisonment. The education provided is seen by them as part of the Church's mission and service to people. Such work of education is not foreign to the concept of evangelisation understood in the broad sense expressed by Paul VI, since evangelisation is linked with the struggle for human advancement, with people's struggle to overcome everything which condemns them to remain on the margin of life, such as famine, disease, illiteracy and poverty.[6]

[4] *The Catholic School on the Threshold of the Third Millennium* no 16
[5] *The Catholic School* no 85
[6] *Evangelisation in the Modern World* no 30

The document, *The Religious Dimension of Education in a Catholic School*, speaks of the situation in which pupils who are not Catholic attend Catholic Schools.

> *Not all students in a Catholic School are members of the Catholic Church, not all are Christians. There are, in fact, countries in which the vast majority of the students are not Catholic, a reality to which Vatican II called attention. The religious freedom and personal conscience of individual students and their families must be respected, and this freedom is explicitly recognised by the Church. On the other hand, a Catholic School cannot relinquish its own freedom to proclaim the Gospel and to offer a formation based on the values to be found in a Christian education; this is its right and duty. To proclaim or to offer is not to impose however; the latter suggests a moral violence which is strictly forbidden, both by the Gospel and by Church law.[7]*

Increasingly in Catholic Schools in the cities of Western Europe there are pupils who are not Catholic and not Christian. The parents of these children and students have chosen a school with a religious foundation rather than one that is run on a secular foundation. Several Bishops' Conferences address the issue. In April 1991 the Bishops' Conference of England and Wales, following a report from the Committee for Other Faiths, commissioned a study on the matter. The final report was presented to the Conference in November 1994. Some minor modifications were made and the report entitled *Catholic Schools and Other Faiths* was then made available with a view to initiating nationwide study and reflection.[8]

---

[7] *The Religious Dimension of Education in a Catholic School* no 6
[8] *Catholic Schools & Other Faiths*

In addition to the full text of the report guidelines for the study and implementation of the report have been drawn up by the Bishops' Conference to help Governors, Headteachers and all in Catholic Schools. The report recognises that *all schools are being challenged by the reality of the multi-faith, multi-cultural society and by new developments in the Church's teaching.* The Guidelines set out measures appropriate for all Catholic Schools, whether they are fully subscribed with Catholic children or are in a situation where they are admitting children of other faiths. The bishops also recommend that Catholic Schools that already admit pupils of other faiths should use the Guidelines as a basis for reviewing their present policies and approach.

The Guidelines are not to be understood as proposing a new concept of 'open enrolment'. Rather, they envisage Catholic Schools who see themselves as serving both the Catholic community and the wider community, with a concern for all people, especially the poor and marginalised, and for the spiritual and moral development of each individual. Such Catholic Schools seek to relate spiritually to all their pupils whether they are Roman Catholic, of other Christian denominations or of other Faiths. They relate to them both from the standpoint of Catholic faith, to which the school must remain true, and from the standpoint of the responsibility which every Catholic School has towards each of its pupils and to the wider world. The circumstances of schools vary considerably. [9]

---

[9] *Guidelines for the Study and Implementation of 'Catholic Schools and Other Faiths'*

17

Partners in a Maintained System

The Church has established schools as a key feature of its Christian service to individuals, families and society. Catholic Schools exist and function in a variety of situations and within different educational systems. In some countries they are part of the national system of education and receive state funding, elsewhere they are independent of the state. The dual system of county and voluntary or denominational schools that exists in England and Wales is not the common system worldwide. It is one that has been gradually established and agreed upon over the years, in discussion and debate between government bodies and denominational groups. County and voluntary schools became part of one public maintained system.

It is an interesting history involving a long struggle to gain a degree of independence. It safeguards some distinctive features of Catholic Schooling:

- the responsibility and control of the school to be in the hands of the Church-appointed governors,
- religious education and worship to be in the tradition of the Catholic Church,
- the right to appoint Catholics teachers and to reserve key leadership roles to practising, committed Catholics,
- to give priority of admission to baptised Catholic children.

Government and local authorities became responsible for the running costs of voluntary schools, with a financial contribution from the Church. Dioceses or religious orders are responsible for meeting a substantial cost of capital expenditure. The remainder is met by public contribution which has increased over the years. Their contribution towards the cost of capital expenditure is still a considerable financial burden for parishes, dioceses and religious orders.

The Bishops of England and Wales recognise this fact but urge the Catholic community to continue supporting the schools.

> *We urge the Catholic community in England and Wales to continue supporting our schools. This means, not least, meeting wherever possible the financial commitment of finding our contribution towards the cost of providing for these institutions. This demonstrates our genuine concern to provide Catholic education for our community, protects our ability to defend and develop its distinctiveness, and puts us in a strong position to argue for the continuation of such provision.*[10]

Increasingly Catholic Schools are seeking some contribution directly from parents to help share this financial cost.

In his address to the Bishops of England and Wales, during their *ad limina* visit, Pope John Paul praised the contribution of Catholic Schools.

> *Within the context of the evangelisation of culture, I wish to acknowledge the fine contribution of your Catholic Schools, both to enriching the faith of the Catholic community and to promoting excellence within civic life in general.*

[10] *Catholic Schools Serving Our Society*

Pause for Reflection

How helpful and useful do you find it to recall that education has always and everywhere been valued not just as some good work among others, but as an essential feature of the Church's mission to people?

While preserving its Catholic identity, how does your school enable pupils and staff to live in a multi-cultural, multi-faith society experienced in and beyond the school in which respect and acceptance of cultural and religious diversity are values to be encouraged?

RICH LEGACY BUT NEW CHALLENGES

The first necessity is a sufficient provision of education adequate for the wants of the poor. It must become universal. Do not rest until you see this want supplied: prefer the establishment of a good school to every other work. Indeed, wherever there may seem to be an opening for a new mission, we should prefer the erection of a school, so arranged to serve temporarily as a chapel, to that of a church without a school. It is the good school that secures the virtuous and edifying congregation.

First Synod of Westminster 1852

The Catholic Hierarchy of England and Wales was restored in 1850. In 1852 the bishops met in synod to consider pastoral priorities for the new situation. The quotation on the previous page sets out the priority they gave to education and Catholic Schools. One hundred and thirty years later a working party produced a report for the Bishops' Conference on the *educative task of the Catholic community* which was published entitled *Signposts and Homecomings*. In the preamble the report touches on some historical developments since 1852.

> *Catholic Schools were founded and developed in response to the needs of the day. The Church became involved in the first half of the 19th century to ensure that the Catholic laity had a grounding in religious knowledge commensurate with their progress in secular education. Most of the schools were parochial and largely under the control of the parish priest or a religious order.*

> *During the period after the war many new Catholic Grammar Schools were founded and the older ones developed and expanded. Their effect was to broaden the horizons of Catholics and move their centre of gravity from the parish and local church. The result of all this – strengthened by comprehensive reorganisation in which Catholic Schools were fully involved – was that the Catholic community is now far more deeply assimilated into the educational system than used to be the case. It might be said that the relationship between the two sectors of the Dual System is one of critical solidarity. Whatever grounds may be found for the development of Catholic Schools in the future they must be closely related to fundamental questions which transcend the process of schooling itself and they must take full account of the developments in the Church and society.[11]*

---

[11] *Signposts and Homecomings* pp 1-3

1852: Schools as a Priority

In the first synod of Westminster, after the restoration of the Catholic hierarchy, the bishops spoke of their desire to build schools before churches. Schools should be the priority. They could be used as chapels for Sunday Mass. In the circumstances of the time the majority of Catholics lived in poverty and great hardship, especially after the influx of so many Irish in the aftermath of the great famine. The Bishops spoke of the urgency of providing a sound education based on religious principles for those deprived of the opportunity of education. They sought to ensure the preservation of Catholic beliefs and practices among Catholic children and the young. Their concerns were both social and religious.

Catholic elementary schools were established, and catered for children from the age of five years until the compulsory school-leaving age. They were very much parish schools, generally situated close to the church, and often served not only temporarily as a chapel but as a social centre catering for the needs of the poor in the parish.

Critical Solidarity

The changes and developments brought about by a variety of Education Acts, lessened the direct control of the parishes. Our schools became more closely associated with the national system of education, while preserving certain rights as voluntary schools sponsored by the Church. With each new Education Act there were serious discussions between church leaders and education ministers. In recent years there has been a constant stream of educational initiatives. A few years ago I was visiting a school. When I arrived the headteacher greeted me warmly but then made a passionate appeal, "No more initiatives please! We have initiative fatigue". The initiatives have continued to pile up. Some are good, some less so, all rather wearying. They invariably mean added work and more stress. Today, as in the past, we are involved in a key pastoral and educational mission of the Church, one that we wish to continue and develop in the new situations that face us today. It is not a mission that we want to see threatened or weakened. In the text *Signposts and Homecomings*, the phrase *critical solidarity* is used several times to indicate the relationship that should exist between Church and government. An enlightening footnote explains what is meant by the phrase.

> The pastoral theology of Vatican II requires the Church to be involved unconditionally with human concerns. Among these concerns education is prominent. So the Christian presence there, is for its own sake. This is the meaning of 'solidarity' in the phrase. However, human progress is of many kinds. It is not an inevitable evolution towards the good. Sometimes it takes false trails. Christians, though themselves involved in human progress, should be able to view it in the perspective of faith and to judge it against their beliefs about the human person and human destiny. This is the force of the word 'critical' in the phrase. It should not be taken wholly negatively since it can involve also leadership and a distinctive contribution to the common human endeavour.[12]

When we speak of our role as one of critical solidarity, we recognise that we work in partnership with government educational agencies. At times, we allow ourselves to be critical of aspects of their policies, not in a purely negative sense, but in the positive sense of defending what we see as key features of sound education. While remaining part of the national system and receiving state funding, we uphold the religious dimension of education within our Christian faith perspective. In this we have rights recognised in legislation and we seek to protect and develop them. A recent Vatican document speaks of the need for *cordial and constructive dialogue* between government bodies and those responsible for Catholic education. Such dialogue should be based on mutual *respect and reciprocal recognition of each other's role.*[13]

---

[12] *Signposts and Homecomings* p 7, note 3

[13] *The Catholic School on the Threshold of the Third Millennium*

At times we have to insist on the proper recognition of our role as key providers of education for a large number of pupils. Often there appears to be a failure to understand and appreciate the voluntary sector and the rights of diocesan and religious trustees. Government initiatives and proposed developments in primary and secondary education can provide many potential opportunities for Catholic Schools. However, they can also present us with significant risks that may jeopardise our vision and practice of sound education, particularly the religious dimension. An example of this is the proposals for 14-19 year olds in secondary schools and colleges. The Catholic Education Service in a letter (2004) warns those involved in Catholic Schools that we have much to offer through excellent education in our Catholic Schools and colleges that we must seize the government's agenda and seek ways to use it to strengthen our sector rather than permit its demise. We have to insist on the proper recognition of our role as key providers of education for a large number of pupils.

In their statement (November 2003) the Bishops expressed concern *that some of the government initiatives in education, even unwittingly, have the effect of undermining that contribution.* We owe our support and our gratitude to those who continue to enter into discussion and debate on our behalf at national and diocesan levels.

Pause for Reflection

What particular potential opportunities or significant risks do you find in some recent government initiatives?

In what ways do you see them as opportunities or risks?

In what way can you take up the task of critical solidarity? Why do you agree, or not agree, with such a stance?

CHALLENGES AND RELIGIOUS CHANGES

The rapid and tumultuous socio-cultural change, increase in numbers, self-affirmation for a consistent period before taking up adult responsibilities, unemployment, the pressures of the consumer society – all contribute to make of youth a world in waiting, not infrequently a world of disenchantment, of boredom, of angst and of marginalisation. Alienation from the Church, or at least diffidence in her regard, lurks in many as a fundamental attitude. Often this reflects lack of spiritual and moral support in the family and weakness in catechesis which they have received. On the other hand, many of them are driven by a strong impetus to find meaning, solidarity, social commitment and even religious experience.

General Directory for Catechesis no 182

A New Cultural, Religious Environment

Catholic Schools not only face challenges that arise out of developments and changes in educational policy. In the 21st century we find ourselves in a vastly different cultural and religious context from that of 1852, or indeed from that of just ten or twenty years ago. The Bishops in 1852 urged the establishment of Catholic Schools to serve the needs of the poor but also as a privileged way of ensuring *the virtuous and edifying congregation*. Today many of the pupils in our schools and their families may well be, and probably are, virtuous and edifying in other respects, but not in that of Church attendance. While numbers decrease at Sunday Mass in parishes, in many places numbers attending our Catholic Schools increase. Clearly they do so for a variety of reasons. What is said in the 1981 report is today even more relevant.

> *No confident assumptions can be made about the religious background even of baptised Catholic pupils entering our schools. Some come from families of strong religious conviction and they give every support to the school and its aims. Others come from families of varying degrees of indifference. It is important to remember this as a significant factor affecting Catholic Schools. Where family and parish support in religious education are lacking a school cannot supply all the deficiencies.[14]*

We are challenged to recognise the changing situations in which our schools now function and to evaluate the positive as well as the negative aspects of such changes. Michael Paul Gallagher, an Irish Jesuit, who lectured in English literature in University College, Dublin, speaks of an occasion when a student came to him to discuss some problem. Having listened to the student, he began by saying, "When I was your age" at which point the student interjected "Father, you were never my age". Taken aback, the priest realised the student meant that he was never nineteen in 1983. Like it or not, we must remember that we are called to serve the young in the first years of the 21st century, in a world and Church very different from

---

[14] *Signposts and Homecomings* p 36

the world and Church in which we were children, teenagers and young adults.

> *One must recognise that, more than ever before, the job of the Catholic School is infinitely more difficult, more complex, since this is a time when Christianity demands to be clothed in new garments, when all manner of changes have been introduced in the Church and in secular life, and particularly, when a pluralist mentality dominates and the Christian Gospel is increasingly pushed to the side-lines.*

> *It is because of this that loyalty to the educational aims of the Catholic School demands constant self-evaluation and return to basic principles, to the motives which inspire the Church's involvement in education. They do not provide a quick answer to contemporary problems, but they give a direction which can begin to solve them.* [15]

Collapse of a Catholic sub-culture

All recent Church documents on education begin with some analysis of the current socio-cultural situation with the implications on family life and religious practice. They speak of youth culture and of the relationship of young people to institutions, including the Church and the faith. It is fairly commonplace to speak of the collapse of a Catholic sub-culture which existed some years ago. It was a time when there was generally a sense of unity of values, purpose and practice, shared between home, school and parish. What was experienced by many as a fairly unified worldview and outlook of faith, has become scattered, pluralist and unsure in its bearings.

Today the coherence between these partners does not exist to anything like the same extent. Family continuity is increasingly rare. Church and parish allegiance, loyalty and commitment are less, often considerably so. The education of children in the faith is a responsibility shared by family, parish and school. Today a great number of families do not pass on the religious tradition to their

---

[15] *The Catholic School* nn 66-67

children. Many leave it to teachers. Parents are not entirely opposed to their children being introduced to the Christian faith in school. For many people the Catholic School is the only experience of Church and Catholicism that they have. However, there is in the lives of many, a separation between Church and family. There is a certain contagious indifference to religion and Christianity, together with a growing individualism found in the culture of consumerism. There are still, of course, religiously committed and practising families.

There is also an important group that can be described as *religiously hesitant people or people on the threshold*. They can be found among the parents and young people, and indeed members of staff in our schools. A recent working party report to the bishops entitled *On The Threshold* encourages interested groups in parishes to reflect on the positive and negative aspects of the religious and spiritual situation of many parents and others in relationship to the Church and the faith. The text starkly acknowledges that *we can no longer assume that people have much, if any, knowledge or experience of Christianity, when they ask for baptism for their children.* In this context it urges a *faithful, sensitive and relevant sharing of the riches of our faith.*[16] The report has much to say concerning the situation of many who seek to have their children admitted to our schools. It encourages a realistic, down-to-earth pastoral approach.

Many now question whether our schools can or do fulfil their mission of promoting and fostering the faith of Catholic pupils. Crudely put, some wonder if we are *getting our money's worth* out of our schools in the sense of committed, practising young people. They see the schools as failing in this key duty. Others acknowledge that this is a more difficult and complex task in a pluralistic, materialistic, as well as multi-cultural and multi-faith society. They argue that a good Catholic School allows the Church to touch and influence the lives of many young people and their families while, at the same time, challenging and offering alternatives to certain views about education and the human person. In this view our schools continue to fulfil the aims set in 1852 but in a different way that

---

[16] *On the Threshold* pp 8-11

responds to the vastly changed cultural and religious situation of today, and can provide opportunities for a *faithful, sensitive and relevant sharing of our faith*. I shall touch on this aspect in a later reflection. However, in this context, Catholics hold different opinions about what can be considered *success* or *failure* in the Church's mission of education through Catholic Schooling today.

In his Dimbleby lecture, some time ago, Rowan Williams, the Archbishop of Canterbury, spoke of this situation and warned against the danger of expecting nothing short of the miraculous from schools. He went on to speak of *damage limitation*. Schools can, I think, provide more than damage limitation, at least with a number of children and young people as well as with some families. The Archbishop supported and challenged Church schools to present the Christian concept of life in which young people can be helped to make choices that are fully human and that enrich their lives and the lives of others. He encouraged them to *give voice* to the Christian story with its inspiration and challenge of making fully human choices. In our secular society schools can provide the space and time for such reflection and discussion; they can *give voice* to the challenging human questions which are often not asked, never mind answered.

Self-evaluation

While we are engaged in serious discussions on a number of new educational proposals, and while we face disturbing issues about faith and religious commitment and practice, we should take the opportunity to clarify our own specific identity and role as Catholic providers of education. If we are to enter into a constructive and cordial dialogue, if our position is one of critical solidarity, then we ourselves must seek to be clear about, and united in, our understanding and delivery of the religious dimension of education within our Christian perspective. If we are to be more confident about the *success* of our schools, as *Catholic*, in the new cultural and religious context in which they are asked to function, we need to reflect more on what we can and should do in the changed and changing conditions of our time. We are reminded, in the Church documents, that Christianity demands to be clothed in new garments, when all manner of changes have been introduced in the Church and secular life, when a pluralist mentality dominates and the Christian gospel is increasingly pushed to the side-lines.[17]

In this context it is useful to bear in mind what John Paul II wrote in his exhortation to the Church in Europe.

Catholic Schools are sometimes the sole means by which the Christian tradition can be presented to those who are distant from it. I encourage the faithful involved in the field of primary and secondary education to persevere in their mission and to bring the light of Christ the Saviour to bear upon their specific educational, scientific and academic activities.[18]

What I present in these pages is not a systematic or in-depth exploration of these issues. Such study belongs in more erudite and detailed tomes. I simply offer some thoughts gathered from Church documents and other writings that touch on some basic principles and on the motivation for the Church's involvement in education. It is my hope that these may help busy teachers to reflect on some issues being raised about Catholic Schools and on key aspects of their service of the young and their families in today's society. I would hope that the quotations and reflections may help those involved in our schools to appreciate the true value of *the job* of the teacher, to see it as more than a job, but also as a mission, a vocation that is of great value to those they seek to educate as well as to the Church and society. I would also hope that these reflections might enable those interested and involved in our schools to articulate, with more confidence and greater clarity, the value of Catholic Schooling and the religious inspiration and motivation for some of the key features which we seek to safeguard and develop in these times of rapid, often disturbing, changes in education, society and the Church.

---

[17] *The Catholic School* no 66
[18] *Ecclesia in Europa* no 59

Pause for Reflection

Does the description of the collapse of a Catholic sub-culture ring true in your experience?

What implications, positive or negative, does this have for what we try to do in our schools?

In what ways can we help pupils to ask and consider the great human questions?
What opportunities for this are there in the various areas of the curriculum?

BASIC PRINCIPLES AND MOTIVATION

The Catholic School is for the human person and of human persons. The person of each individual human being, in his or her material and spiritual needs, is at the heart of Christ's teaching: this is why the promotion of the human person is the goal of the Catholic School.

John Paul II

The document *The Catholic School on the Threshold of the Third Millennium*, in which the quotation from John Paul II occurs, goes on to say:

> *There is a tendency to forget that education always presupposes and involves a definite concept of the person and life. To claim neutrality for schools signifies in practice, more times than not, banning all reference to religion from the cultural and educational field, whereas a correct pedagogical approach ought to be open to the more decisive sphere of ultimate objectives, attending not only to **how** but also to **why**, overcoming any misunderstanding as regards the claim to neutrality in education, restoring to the educational process the unity which saves it from dispersion amid the meandering of knowledge and acquired facts, and focuses on the human person in his or her integral, transcendent, historic identity. With its educational project inspired by the Gospel, the Catholic School takes up this challenge.[19]*

The Dignity of the Person

At the very heart of the educational mission of Catholic Schools is the belief in the God-given dignity of each and every person and in the significance, value and worth of all human life. This concept of education flows from the Christian faith and belief in the human person created in the image of God. In this faith we profess that every single human being is uniquely created in love by God and is destined to share in the life and love of the Father, Son and Holy Spirit. We acknowledge that, numbed and limited by sinfulness, we spoil God's creation. We believe that in the death and resurrection of Christ we can gain forgiveness and reconciliation with God and each other. We look forward to life beyond the grave.

At first sight these somewhat high-flown theological concepts may seem very far removed from the busy daily task of teaching and organising life in our schools. It may be far from easy to believe in God's loving act of creation of each human being when we think of

---

[19] *The Catholic School on the Threshold of the Third Millennium* nn 9&10

that restless, troublesome Johnny or Mary whose stubborn aggression disturbs our classes.

The perception of Christian acceptance and forgiveness as a lived experience in the school may not be readily recognised by some pupils. Some may wonder if past faults can ever be forgotten or forgiven, at least by some teachers, despite all the talk about, and celebration of, the sacrament or services of reconciliation. Some teachers do seem to have in their mind a database of faults in which nothing is deleted but to which a great deal is added. Misdemeanours are stored and frequently downloaded and presented to the recalcitrant culprit who may even be reminded that some years before him or her it was the same story with their sibling.

Of course, misdemeanours will be recorded and the troublesome will be reprimanded. At the same time support and guidance will be offered and attempts to improve behaviour will be noted and rewarded. This happens daily in our schools. The process can sap energy as well as give some well-deserved satisfaction. A Christian theology of creation or reconciliation will hardly be uppermost in our minds as we go about this task. Yet the belief that God created each and every human being and that we can play a part in the education of the person, enabling them to grow and develop, is the very heart of our mission in schools.

There are also times when, through symbol, ritual and prayer, we support and comfort pupils, families and staff at particular moments of grief, particularly at the loss of a loved-one, and together we profess our belief that death is not the end for those who have gone or for those who are left.

Living out our Beliefs and Values

Properly understood and reflected on, what we believe has immediate and direct relevance to all we strive to do in our schools. It can and should motivate, inspire and challenge us in such matters as:

- a welcoming ethos
- a strong pastoral care system
- supportive and healthy relationships with all involved in school
- a balanced system of discipline, rewards and sanctions that acknowledge faults yet is open to acceptance
- the possibility of starting anew with guidance and support
- a broad and balanced curriculum that addresses the needs and capabilities of all pupils.

Our beliefs also challenge us to provide opportunities in which pupils and staff can have time and space to reflect, in ways suited to their age and abilities, on the great questions concerning the significance of human life, on the rights and responsibilities of each individual and the community. All areas of the curriculum, some more than others, offer opportunities for this, not just Religious Education. In the imparting of knowledge and skills we are challenged to bear in mind that

> the various school subjects do not present only knowledge to be attained, but also values to be acquired and truths to be discovered.[20]

Assemblies and other forms of worship and prayer can open the pupils and staff to such reflection. In this way we take to heart Pope John Paul's message to Italian teachers:

> The person of each and every human being, in his or her material and spiritual needs, is at the heart of Christ's teaching; that is why the promotion of the human person is the goal of the Catholic School.

[20] *The Catholic School on the Threshold of the Third Millennium* 14

basic principles and motivation

Our Theology

Underpinning and motivating all that we do in the mission of Catholic education is a faith perspective about what it means to be human and how best we can educate children and young people to fulfil their human potential. This is a distinctive feature of Catholic Schools. While other schools may show the same care and concern for pupils, their motivation for doing so may be different. Our philosophy of education grows out of our Christian faith and understanding of the human person. In his book *Educating for Life*, Thomas Groome, the well-known religious educator in Boston College, sees the ultimate foundations of education as *spiritual*. By *spiritual* he means

> the operative commitments from a faith perspective that undergrid and permeate their educating – the deep-down things that persons really believe in and that shape how they educate.[21]

Certainly in the daily hustle and bustle of school life there is little opportunity for unpacking and reflecting on these deep-down things. For this to happen it is necessary to provide the occasional day or part of a day when an atmosphere can be created which is conducive to such individual reflection and sharing among staff. Talk of a philosophy or theology of education may not come easily to most of us, but we all need time when we can pause and reflect on why we do the job, what it is really all about and, when possible, to reflect together with colleagues. Recently I came across a quotation from G K Chesterton that I think brings this home quite forcefully.

> Every education teaches a philosophy, if not by dogma, then by suggestion, by implication, by atmosphere. Every part of that education has a connection with every other part. If it does not all combine to convey some general view of life it is not education at all.[22]

---

[21] T Groome *Educating for Life*
[22] G K Chesterton *The Common Man* p 167

Teachers as Educators

Church documents stress the fact that teachers are educators. That may seem tautological. However, the statement makes a profound point:

> *The teacher is not simply a professional person who systematically transmits a body of knowledge in the context of a school; 'teacher' is to be understood as 'educator' - one who helps to form human persons.*[23]

The teacher's task is not confined to the delivery of his or her area of the curriculum. Of course, a sound knowledge of the subject and the ability to help pupils learn within that curriculum area is a fundamental part of the teacher's task. This is one of the main reasons why a teacher is employed by the school and one of the key ways in which he or she helps the school be appreciated by pupils and parents. Church documents remind us that, as well as through lesson delivery, a teacher influences pupils in all sorts of ways, particularly through relationships and guidance and support offered in and out of the classroom. Teachers do not simply deal with the intellectual dimension of the person, but are also involved at different times and in different ways in the cultural, emotional, spiritual, religious dimensions. Another document expresses it in this way:

> *The purpose of instruction at school is education: the development of persons from within, freeing them from that conditioning which prevents them from becoming fully integrated human beings. The school's educational programme is intentionally directed to the growth of the whole person.*[24]

Again we are reminded that the purpose of *instruction* in schools, is *education*. The texts describe education as being concerned with enabling pupils to become *fully integrated human beings*, often by enabling them to overcome conditions which prevent them from learning and from developing as integrated human beings. Later I shall look at what recent documents say about different types or

---

[23] *Lay Catholics in School: Witnesses to Faith* no 16
[24] *The Catholic School* no 29

categories of pupils in our schools today, and about conditions that restrict their full development as integrated human beings. Our schools no longer cater only for the academically bright pupils, or pupils from secure and loving homes, or only for the committed and practising Catholic. We are all deeply conscious of some of the harrowing situations in which some of our pupils live and the impact this has on their lives and their attitude to school. It is because of this that we are wary of crude league tables.

Much of what we now do in schools may seem to be more akin to social work than teaching, but this is seen as an essential feature of *education* as spelt out in Church documents and the mission of evangelisation which, as we have seen in the words of Paul VI, is linked with the struggle for human advancement, with the struggle to overcome everything that condemns people to remain on the margins of life. In our schools we play a vital, if limited, part in evangelisation understood in this way.

The Whole Person

The documents constantly speak of sound education as addressing the whole person. They stress that attention must be given to all pupils, the high-flyers and those with special needs who should in no way be overlooked in the desire to achieve points on the league tables. Cardinal Hume in an address to teachers reminded them that the human person is at the heart of Catholic teaching and that every person is to be valued as God's creation; after the example of Jesus we should be available to all. The Church's teaching does not fragment the person or culture into distinct, unrelated parts; it does not focus on some particular aspect such as the intellectual or religious, or overstress the spiritual to the neglect of the physical and emotional. Individual teachers cannot address or meet all of these needs and demands all of the time. There will be occasions when they can attend to some of these for individuals or groups of pupils. However, the overall management of the school should see that there are staff members with the appropriate skills and relationships who can attend to the great variety of needs, among pupils and families.

We need to remember why we founded Catholic Schools. The establishment of the majority of the Catholic educational institutions has responded to the needs of the socially and economically disadvantaged. The names of outstanding saints who were educators of the young are listed in this context, among them Jean Baptiste de La Salle and Don Bosco.[25]

The 1981 report to the Bishops stressed this same point.

One of the paradoxical strengths of the Church is that it is in every sense Catholic, it is for the weak and for the strong, for those who fail as well as for those who succeed, for sinners as well as for saints. It could be the ability of our schools to be Catholic, in that sense, that they could have something unique to contribute to education in our country as well as in their being signs of living and urgent faith.[26]

An Educating Community

Much is made of the community dimension of the Catholic School in Church documents.

While respecting individual roles, the community dimension should be fostered, since it is one of the most enriching developments for the contemporary school. It is also helpful to bear in mind, in harmony with the Second Vatican Council, that this community dimension in the Catholic School is not a merely sociological category; it has a theological foundation as well. The educating community, taken as a whole, is thus called to further the objective of a school as a place of complete formation through interpersonal relations.[27]

Vatican II spoke of the school as a community rather than as an institution and urged creating within the school *an atmosphere enlivened by the gospel spirit of freedom and love.* The theological basis for community, as a characteristic of a Catholic School, is to be found especially in the Christian belief in God as Trinity - Father, Son and Spirit.

---

[25] *The Catholic School on the Threshold of the Third Millennium* no 15
[26] *Signposts and Homecomings* p 5
[27] *The Catholic School on the Threshold of the Third Millennium* no 18

When we express our belief that each human being is created in the image of God, we do not refer simply to a spiritual dimension of the person. We declare that, created in the image of God who is Trinity, each human being is of equal dignity and develops fully as a person within a community of persons, in relationships of respect and love with other persons. It is for this reason that great importance is given to the community dimension in our schools, to the creation of a climate in which individuals are encouraged and enabled to grow and develop personally and socially.[28] The prime responsibility for creating this climate rests with the teachers as individuals and as an educating community. We more often speak of being a *team* but the term *educating community* has deeper and religious connotations.

In this context of an educating community, frequent mention is made of the importance of collaboration with parents, of the need to foster initiatives which encourage their commitment to what the school does, while offering at the same time the support which families need. It must be remembered, of course, that teachers with their professional skills help parents in their roles as the primary and natural educators of their children. There is praise and encouragement for *the unpretentious yet caring and sensitive help offered in those cases, more and more numerous above all in wealthy nations, of families which are fragile or have broken up.*[29]

Our Model Christ

All that has been said about a Catholic School can be succinctly summarised in a sentence from a recent Church document.

> *The integral education of the human person through a clear educational project of which Christ is the foundation.*[30]

The focus of all our educational endeavours is each individual pupil with their own variety of needs and capabilities. We look to the needs of the whole person: intellectual, physical, moral, emotional, spiritual and religious. Within this process individual members of

---

[28] *General Directory for Catechesis* n 100
[29] *The Catholic School on the Threshold of the Third Millennium* no 5
[30] *The Catholic School on the Threshold of the Third Millennium* no 4

staff will have specific roles and will concentrate on particular aspects. But as a team, an educating community, with a shared vision, we seek to attend to all aspects, helping each pupil develop and mature. In this we have Jesus as our Model. There is a sentence from the document *The Catholic School* which I frequently use and it is one which often appeals to staff.

> *The Catholic character of a Catholic School is rooted in the Christian concept of life which is centred on Jesus Christ: he is the one who ennobles people, gives meaning to human life, and is the Model which the Catholic School offers its pupils.*[31]

Our task is that of ennobling, enriching the lives of each child and young person. We do so through our personal relationships and in the way we organise and manage the entire life of the school. Care should be taken that nothing is done by individual staff members or by the general system of discipline and sanctions that demeans or belittles personal dignity. I conclude this section with some thoughts from the document *The Catholic School*.

> *The Catholic School loses its purpose without constant reference to the Gospel. It derives its necessary energy for all its educational work from Christ. It thus creates in the school community an atmosphere permeated with the Gospel spirit of freedom and love. In this setting pupils will experience their dignity as persons before they know its definition. In this way the school is faithful to the claims of the person and of God, it makes its own contribution to human liberation.*[32]

---

[31] *The Catholic School on the Threshold of the Third Millennium* no 35
[32] *The Catholic School* no 55

43

Pause for Reflection

Which of the principles or motivations given for education in these pages has most inspired you? Most challenged you?

Which do you experience most in your school? Which less?

Do you find reference to Christian beliefs and theology helpful or less than helpful, in what ways?

Do you recognise your school as an 'educative community'?
In what ways do you experience this sense of community?

What passages from the gospels speak most powerfully to you about the educator?

SERVING A VARIETY OF NEEDS

First and foremost, we must recognise the contribution the Catholic School makes to the evangelising mission of the Church throughout the world, including areas in which no other form of pastoral work is possible. Moreover, in spite of numerous obstacles, the Catholic School has continued to share responsibility for the social and cultural development of different communities and peoples to which it belongs, participating in their joys and hopes, their sufferings and difficulties, their efforts to achieve genuine human and communitarian progress. In this respect, mention must be made of the invaluable services of the Catholic School to the spiritual and material development of people who are less fortunate.

The Catholic School on the Threshold of the Third Millennium no 5

Many Different Situations

Any school that has existed in the one area for some thirty, forty or fifty years will no doubt have experienced a great deal of development and changes in that area. These will have had some impact on the school. Among factors that will have affected many schools are population shifts, urban redevelopment, growing unemployment, falling birth rates, decline in religious practice and commitment, the increasing breakdown in family life, a multi-cultural and multi-faith society that may now be much in evidence within the neighbourhood of the school. As a result, many will have been involved in some reorganisation or amalgamation.

For many schools there has been and still is a continuing history of adaptation and change as they face the challenges of serving the needs of pupils and families and of addressing the demands of the new situations within the locality. We talk frequently of *The* Catholic School. This allows us to refer to a set of basic principles and characteristics that should be among the distinctive features of the education we seek to provide in all our primary and secondary Catholic Schools. Yet, in fact, *the* Catholic School does not in reality exist. *This* Catholic School of St James, Hartlepool, and *this* Catholic School of Our Lady in Hackney exist. These schools and all our schools exist in different and changing situations.

Factors that impinge on our mission

When we talk of *the* Catholic School, we talk in abstract, of a school that is without real people and that is not situated in a particular locality. When we consider the educational and pastoral service each school can provide we have to consider such factors as:

- The economic situation
- The social situation
- The cultural situation
- The ethnic and racial situation
- The religious situation.

It is within a specific context that each of our schools is called to serve children, young people, their families and the community of the locality.

Even within the one diocese, schools serve pupils and families of very different social and cultural backgrounds. Recently I touched on this when addressing Deputy Heads of primary schools in a large diocese. At one point I asked them to turn to a few people sitting near them and just say something about the particular situation of their own school and how these factors impinged on them. Naturally from such a large diocese there was a great variety of situations. I could overhear some discussion from those in the front row, and found what was being said reinforced very powerfully the point that I was rather hesitantly making. So much so that I asked them to share with the whole group their descriptions of the areas served by their schools. One was in a pleasant leafy suburb with a large number of professional people, mostly white, with a fairly large percentage of practising committed Catholics. The second served an urban locality, a culturally and racially mixed area. The pupils came from a variety of cultures, for many, English was a second language. Many were Catholics, with a growing number of pupils from faiths, other than Christian, applying for places. There was considerable unemployment and poverty. The third served an area partly urban, partly rural with pupils of different social backgrounds, with many non-practising Catholic families, and a good number of pupils who were not Catholic.

In some places Catholic Schools are oversubscribed with many more families applying than there are places; even baptised Catholics cannot easily find a place in a local Catholic primary or nearby Catholic secondary school. Elsewhere, for a variety of reasons, schools are under-subscribed with vacant places and a fair percentage of pupils who are not Catholic. In some cities, families of faiths other than Christian are requesting places for their children in Catholic Schools because of the religious ethos. These are only some features of the diversity of situations in which our schools seek to fulfil their mission of serving the young in today's rapidly changing society.

Particular people in a particular place

It is in a particular place, in a particular locality or, in the case of many secondary schools, in a wider area with pupils from a variety of localities that our schools seek to live out the Church's mission of education. While all Catholic Schools should adhere to the basic principles and motivation for Catholic Schooling, each will seek to fulfil its mission in *this* place and with *these* people. The Christian motivation for this can be found in our belief and theology of the Incarnation. Jesus became one of us in a particular time and a particular place. The Incarnation is the acceptance of the human condition along with all its implications. As was said in the opening quotation for this section, *it is in this way that we, share responsibility for the social and cultural development of different communities and peoples, participating in their joys and hopes, their sufferings and difficulties, their effort to achieve genuine human and communitarian progress.*

Too often I think that we apply these directives in Church documents to the *developing* countries, to what we used to term the *foreign missions*. We need also to realise that they can and do speak to the situations in some of the large council estates, to the social and culture mix of many of the localities in which a good number of our schools are called to serve on behalf of the Church. We too work in mission territory in which the school, in the name of the Church, goes out, is sent out to share and participate in the social, cultural, spiritual and material development of people, especially the disadvantaged in our society.

The word *mission* derives from the Latin verb *mitto*, noun *missio* – to send, despatch, to make to go. We go out to touch and enrich the lives of people where they are. This is an essential aspect of the educational and pastoral mission of our Catholic Schools that we may need to reflect on seriously and prayerfully. In evaluating the *success* of our schools, as Catholic Schools, we must bear in mind this context and the underpinning belief and theology of Incarnation which should have a bearing on our judgement.

A meeting point for the problems of today

When we consider some of the contexts, it is evident that our pupils come from a variety of experiences and cultural and social backgrounds. Consequently they have a whole range of physical, intellectual, social, emotional, spiritual and religious needs. While we seek to provide the knowledge and skills necessary for life and work, we recognise a great variety of capabilities and, often, all sorts of obstacles that prevent both learning and full human development. Recent Church documents are very much aware of this and speak, at times, in terms that may seem rather drastic and dramatic. Yet most teachers can identify with much of what is stated.

The problems of the world, and society outside the school, affect the pupils, their families and the members of staff. While we seek to create a *safe place* for the young, we cannot provide a clinically sealed area. The following quotation paints what may seem a rather bleak picture of the situations of many children and young people.

> *The Catholic School is confronted with children and young people who shun effort, are incapable of self-sacrifice and perseverance, who lack authentic models to guide them, often even in their own families. In an increasing number of instances they are not only indifferent and non-practising, but also totally lacking in religious and moral formation. On the part of many pupils and families there is a profound apathy where moral and religious formation is concerned.[33]*

We may find the words *incapable of* too strong; certainly some find it difficult to show self-sacrifice and perseverance. We are aware of some of the unhealthy social and family contexts, discouraging many young people from developing and displaying such values and strengths. We are also aware of the lack of religious and moral formation in many who attend our schools and of the apathy in regard to religion and morals, especially amongst some of our older pupils. While all this can bring about *pedagogical tiredness*, it can also motivate teachers and bring home to them the value of the task

---

[33] *The Catholic School on the Threshold of the Third Millennium* no 6

of educating, of helping to form and develop, however hesitantly and with whatever difficulties, a human person. The text sees the Catholic School as, *a genuine instrument of the Church, a place of real and specific pastoral ministry...the privileged environment in which Christian education is carried out.*[34] It speaks of the many parts of the world in which material poverty prevents many young people from having access to formal education and goes on to specify *new forms of poverty* that challenge Catholic Schools, in parts of the world, including the more *developed* societies such as ours. Just as many saintly educators in the past sought to educate the poor, the same mission is needed and called for today.

> *Young people can be found again among those who have lost all sense of meaning in life and lack any type of inspiring ideal, those to whom no values are proposed and who do not know the beauty of faith, who come from families which are broken and incapable of love, often living in situations of material and spiritual poverty, slaves to the new idols of a society which, not infrequently, promises them only a future of un-employment and marginalisation. To these new poor the Catholic School turns in a spirit of love by offering the opportunity of an education, of training for a job, of human and Christian formation.*[35]

I see this last sentence as a powerful rallying cry to anyone involved in the life of our schools, particularly in difficult and disadvantaged localities, who may feel tired and discouraged. The Church acknowledges and appreciates the difficulties and the joys that are part and parcel of the mission of education in such situations. The Church gives us a strong exhortation to continue our work. Also in areas where there is not so much deprivation our schools are challenged to meet and address the needs of students who, while materially comfortable, know something of the lack of family love and support and who can know spiritual poverty.

---

[34] *The Catholic School on the Threshold of the Third Millennium* no 11
[35] *The Catholic School on the Threshold of the Third Millennium* no 15

A Welcoming Environment

The document *Spiritual and Moral Development Across the Curriculum* addresses the same issues. In tackling such a sensitive and personal area as spiritual development it states:

> *It is crucial that we are keenly aware of all that works against our aims. Many of our pupils come from secure, happy homes, and are well supported by their parish community. For them the shared values of home, parish and school create an environment of trust and openness. However, some of our pupils bring to school experiences, which have seriously damaged their capacity or readiness to develop a sense of self-worth or of the value of life and the world around them. Many of them are deeply marked by distrust, if not hatred, of themselves and of others. They are already cynical about anything which appears to be good or wholesome, and highly skilled at hiding their vulnerability and sensitivity.*[36]

Here again we have a rather sombre, dramatic picture. Most teachers recognise some of these characteristics among a number of their pupils. The same document stresses the importance of creating a healthy and safe school environment, inspired and challenged by the Christian faith vision of life and the person.

> *There can be no doubt of the importance of the environment we create for our pupils if they are ever to move out of the imprisonment of such experiences. And, in this environment, acceptance, respect and love are essential. Creating and maintaining this safe place is, for teachers, both difficult and demanding, particularly for those who may themselves be trying to come to terms with similar experiences.*[37]

It is certainly a difficult yet rewarding task to help the young *to move out of the imprisonment of such experiences*. This is an essential feature of education as described in the document *The Catholic School* which I quoted earlier: *the development of persons from within, freeing them from that conditioning which prevents them*

---

[36] *Spiritual & Moral Development Across the Curriculum* n 35
[37] *Spiritual & Moral Development Across the Curriculum* n 36

from becoming fully integrated human beings. Again, a Christian theology of creation, belief in the unique creation by God of each person, can provide an underlying motivation for teachers as educators to continue to play their important, if limited, part in the creation and development of a person. After parenting, this is a vital and important mission.

A Supportive Community

In their attitude towards pupils, staff can affirm and encourage those already supported by their families and who take part in parish life. They can help heal the more fragile and disadvantaged pupils. Welcoming and cheerful secretarial staff and those who serve in school kitchens can and do play an important role in this regard for pupils, families and teaching staff. Much will be done through the pastoral care system in the school. When speaking of the promotion of faith in pupils *The General Catechetical Directory* stresses the importance of sound pastoral care:

> *It should be remembered that the most successful catechesis (education to and in the faith) is that which is given in the context of wider pastoral care of young people, especially when it addresses the problems affecting their lives.*[38]

In this context a saying of Michael Paul Gallagher is very apt: *When self-worth is wounded, a whole language of faith – human and religious – may stutter and fall silent, unreadiness for revelation can have roots in this area of a person's life.*[39]

A welcoming, accepting and caring atmosphere in the school and the trust and encouragement of teachers and other staff can help open the less self-assured pupils to a fuller faith and belief in themselves, others and God. If we can help pupils believe more in themselves and others, if we can enable them to smile more and be more confident, then we have taken them on a worthwhile, even if limited, journey of faith.

---

[38] *General Directory for Catechesis* n 184
[39] M P Gallagher *Free to Believe* p 94

Tensions and Dilemmas

In today's climate of market forces and league tables, it is not easy to take up the challenge of education as outlined in Church documents. Of course, the academic development of all children is an important aspect of any sound education. It is the right of all children to be encouraged to develop their capabilities to the maximum possible for them. However, there is the very real danger that some schools will be almost entirely driven by the desire to play the market by scoring maximum points in the league tables of academic success. In doing so the needs of some pupils, especially of the most vulnerable and weak, may be overlooked. To accept and keep academically weaker pupils, and those who may be alienated and somewhat troublesome and without healthy family support, runs the risk of scoring low on the league tables of *success*. How we approach and tackle such tensions and dilemmas may well have practical consequences in the way parents and others see and judge the school.

Some parents stress the need for clear and measurable academic success in examination results. In their eyes this is necessary to enhance their children's opportunities in other spheres of education and later in life. Failure to meet such aspirations runs the risk of falling numbers of pupils if parents decide to choose other, apparently more *successful*, schools for their children. Other parents rate more highly a welcoming, friendly, safe environment in which their children will be happy and content and encouraged to learn according to their abilities, to feel at home and have a sense of belonging within the school community. Trying to meet the aspirations of parents, leaves Headteachers and Governors with the dilemma that is aptly expressed by Professor Gerald Grace: *a competitive market culture in schooling is making it much more difficult to be in the service of the poor, the troublesome, the alienated and the powerless.*[40]

It is not only Headteachers and Governors who face these tensions and dilemmas. Class teachers in primary schools and teachers of a

---

[40]   G Grace *The Future of the Catholic School*

particular subject area in secondary schools may bemoan the presence of pupils in their classes who will lower their overall success in public examinations and their ranking on the league tables. All very understandable and at times it may well be best for pupils and the whole class if they could be placed in another group. That is not always possible and may not be desirable.

These are some of the tensions and dilemmas that face those involved in running our Catholic Schools and in those faced with making a choice of school for their children. It can be difficult to hold in proper balance the need to be recognised by parents and others as *a good and successful school* and, on the other hand, to be *a school for all – for the weak and for the strong.* The 1981 report already quoted reminds us that this could be a unique contribution that we could offer to education in our country.[41]

I conclude this section with what I consider a relevant quotation from the Catholic Education Service document *The Common Good in Education.*

> *The pursuit of excellence is intrinsically good when it is seen as an integral part of the spiritual quest and not simply as a matter of competitive league tables. Competition is, of itself, neither good nor evil, but when it is used to brand children in a way that limits their freedom or potential, it is damaging to human flourishing. It also carries the danger of communicating to children and young people – and, indeed, to the wider community – that a person's value is measured solely in terms of academic, sporting or financial success.*[42]

The text also sees education not as *a commodity offered for sale*, but as *the service of others rather than the service of self.* It dislikes the substitution of the term *public provider* for *public servant* because this appears to undermine the sense of vocation that most teachers have.

---

[41] *Signposts and Homecomings* p 5
[42] *The Common Good in Education* p 13

Pause for Reflection

How would you describe the economic, social, cultural, ethnic, religious situation of your school?

How do these factors impinge on what you try to do in education within the context of your Catholic School?

What is your reaction to some of the quotations concerning the situations of pupils in schools today?

Can you recognise features of your own pupils in such descriptions?

What inspiration or challenge do you find in these reflections?

In what ways can the school help pupils move out of the imprisonment of such experiences?

What are the main tensions or dilemmas which you experience in seeking to be a good school founded on Christian principles and Gospel values?

FAITH EDUCATION: POTENTIAL & LIMITATIONS

It should be no surprise that young people bring with them into the classroom what they see and hear in the world around them, along with the impressions gained from the world of mass media. Perhaps some have become indifferent and insensitive. The school curriculum, as such, does not take these attitudes into account, but teachers are very aware of them. With kindness and understanding, they will accept the students as they are, helping them to see that doubt and indifference are common phenomena, and that the reasons for this are readily understandable. But they will invite students in a friendly manner to seek and discover together the message of the Gospel, the source of joy and peace. The teachers' attitudes and behaviour should be those of one preparing the soil. They then can add their own spiritual lives, and the prayers they offer for the students entrusted to them.

The Religious Dimension of Education in a Catholic School no 71

Religious and Spiritual Needs

The Church document on the religious dimension of education in our schools reminds us that the school *assists and promotes faith education.*[43] As we have seen in a previous reflection, in 1852 the Bishops urged the Catholic community to give priority to the education of children and young people especially the poorest. They also spoke of the needs of *other classes no less dear to us.* They urged that the education provided in our Catholic Schools should, within the limitations of resources, be as good as that provided in any other school. In addition to such *secular instruction* the Catholic School should address the religious and spiritual needs of the pupils: *while we thus wish to promote a secular instruction equal to what others offer, we consider sound faith, virtue and piety by far the most important elements of education.* Within our Catholic Schools education should also be *education in sound faith and virtuous morals.* Their concern was to provide a sound education for all Catholic children, an education which sought to preserve and promote the faith of pupils. They preferred the erection of a school to that of a church: *For the building raised of living stones, the spiritual sanctuary of the Church, is of far greater importance than the temple made by hands. And it is the good school that secures the virtuous and edifying congregation.*

We are now aware that a large number of pupils in our schools do not come from committed and practising Catholic families. Some Catholics may wonder whether we can and are fulfilling the mission urged on us by the Bishops in 1852. Others would say that we are fulfilling that mission in our different cultural and religious society. It may now be more of a question of the school providing for many pupils an environment in which the Christian faith can be *presented and, within limits, promoted.* Some time ago, particularly when there was a fairly cohesive Catholic sub-culture, schools may have been able to provide an environment in which the faith experienced in the home and strengthened in the parish could be *preserved and deepened.* Like it or not, long since gone are the days when the

---

[43] *The Religious Dimension of Education in a Catholic School* no 69

majority of pupils and their families were actively committed to the faith. The 1981 report already highlighted this situation: *no confident assumptions can be made about the religious background even of baptised Catholic pupils entering our schools.*

Some limitations in the school context

In this context the school can play an important yet limited part in the faith education of children and young people. Michael Paul Gallagher reminds us that in the matter of faith and religious development the school is a relatively secondary influence:

> *The religious formation offered by the school is inevitably influenced by the home background and so it depends greatly on whether the home is co-operative or non co-operative. And a home can be saying all the right things, but the stronger non-verbal message is that faith is not too vital for the real concerns of life. It needs to be recognised that the school is a relatively secondary influence in the religious search of the young. In terms of contact hours, this is obvious (and in terms of such measurement the school may be more central than the parish).* [44]

I have already touched on this issue when reflecting on the new cultural and religious environment, on the collapse of the Catholic sub-culture and when reflecting on the variety of needs among pupils and their families. Here I wish to reflect more specifically on the potential and limitations of school in helping to promote faith education of pupils in such a context.

Clearly the school works within certain limitations. The amount of time in school is one such limitation. Faith develops over the whole of a person's life. School years cover at most fifteen years of life. Quite a while ago now an educational document was published entitled 15,000 Hours. [45] The title was a reminder that out of a life time the sum total of time spent at school could amount to 15,000 hours, relatively speaking not a lot. However, the hours and years

---

[44] M P Gallagher S J *Help My Unbelief* p 88

[45] Rutter M et al *15000 Hours*

spent in school occur at a very important period of life when young people are very impressionable and open to the influence of adults who are significant in their lives. Another factor that affects the way the school can influence faith education of pupils is the experience and background of the home and locality in which they live. Again the 1981 report points out *where family and parish support in religious education are lacking a school cannot supply all the deficiencies.* It also has to be borne in mind that, particularly during the adolescent years, young people begin to question the beliefs and values, religious or not, held by parents and other significant people. Even committed, practising and caring parents are often faced with sons and daughters whose questioning and way of life seem to rebel against the parents' deeply held beliefs and values.

The Catholic School would no longer deserve this title if, no matter how much it shone for its high level of teaching in non-religious matters, there were justification for reproaching it for negligence or deviation in strictly religious education. Let it not be said that such education will always be given implicitly and indirectly.

While Catholic establishments should respect freedom of conscience, that is to say avoid burdening consciences from without by exerting physical or moral pressure, especially in the case of the religious activity of adolescents, they still have the grave duty to offer a religious training suited to the often widely varying religious situations of the pupils.[46]

An attitude of Respect and Dialogue

Teachers and parents have to acknowledge and try to understand the reasons why young people experience and express doubt and indifference. This may not come easily to some of us but it is necessary if there is to be any true exchange of views and sharing of faith and values. A Vatican text points out some attitudes necessary for this task: affection, tact, understanding, serenity of spirit, a

---

[46] John Paul II Catechesis in our Time no 69

balanced judgement, patience in listening, prudence in the way we respond and availability to meet and spend time with the young.[47] All members of staff can be open to the young in this way. It is an important aspect of the work of chaplains, class teachers in primary schools and form tutors in secondary schools, as well as others more involved in pastoral care. If we are to help the young develop in Christian faith we may be critical of the negative aspects of their life and culture, expressing our views with honesty and respect. At the same time, together with them, we must try to recognise, understand and bless what is good in their lifestyle and culture. If we wish to share our faith and attract them to our Christian faith, we must present it in such a way that they can recognise that it addresses their questions and problems, their hopes and aspirations. One writer has expressed the opinion that faith is difficult for many people, especially the young, not because of its intellectual demand or because of the personal sacrifices it requires. In his view *the problem is that faith seems less than we are, smaller than life, unrelated to love and insufficient for hope.*[48] Yet properly understood and presented, our Christian faith and beliefs speak most profoundly about the richness and values of life, love and hope.[49] A passage from Vatican II is particularly relevant to this reflection:

> *We can justly consider*
> *that the future lies in the hands of those*
> *who are strong enough to provide*
> *coming generations with reasons*
> *for living and hoping.*[50]

---

[47] *The Religious Dimension of Education in a Catholic School* no 96
[48] A Padovani *Free to be Faithful*
[49] See *Soil for the Seed* pp 183 185
[50] *The Church in the Modern World* no 31

Accompanying the Young in Faith

I often find it useful when discussing this issue with staff and Governors to reflect with them on what is said in the introduction to *The Rite of the Baptism of Children*. In that text several relevant points to this reflection are made. I summarise and list here the first four sections of the introduction.

1. Children or infants cannot profess a personal faith.

2. From the earliest times they are baptised in the faith of the Church proclaimed by parents and godparents.

3. Children must be later formed in the faith in which they were baptised. Christian formation seeks to lead them gradually to learn God's plan in Christ so that they may ultimately accept for themselves the faith in which they were baptised.

4. The people of God, that is the Church, made present in the local community, has an important part to play. Before and after the celebration the child has the right to the love and help of the community.

This opens up a number of reflections. Young children cannot profess a personal faith; they experience and gradually express something of the faith of the adults who play a significant part in their lives: parents, grandparents, relatives and teachers. They absorb the love, trust and the faith of these important people for them. They gradually learn and understand, in a way suited to their age and capabilities, something of that faith. Ultimately, however, they will choose for themselves and come to accept or reject, wholly or in part, the faith others may have tried to share with them. Many will make their own the faith they have grown up in, they will cultivate and deepen it within their own experiences of life. Many will question, even reject or move away from the faith, experienced and taught in the family and school. Of course, we are aware that many children do not experience much of the Christian faith in the home. Even those who have such an experience of shared Christian faith and beliefs, will come to a point in life when they will decide for themselves.

This has been called the period of *searching faith* when the young person cannot live by any person's faith but his or her own. For many adults this can be seen as a difficult, troublesome time. Yet it is an essential, crucial stage in the journey of faith. It is a time when the young have need for patient, understanding companions on the road. This is a mission open particularly to parents and teachers, though for some young people it is not easy to confide in them. In this situation the chaplaincy team and pastoral care staff have much to offer. *The General Directory for Catechesis* reminds us, as I quoted earlier, that the most successful catechesis, education to and in faith, is that offered within a broader pastoral care for young people which addresses the problems affecting their lives.

Those who were baptised in infancy, or as young children, were baptised in the faith of the Church. We are reminded that, before and after the ceremony, the child has the right to the love and help of the community. Our Catholic Schools are one important aspect of the love and help offered by the community. Even if the parents have not been totally faithful to the promises made during the ceremony, it can be argued that we, the community, should seek to be faithful to our commitments taken on at the baptism of the child. There is considerable debate among Catholics about the criteria that should be set for the baptism of a child, for example the strength of the requirement that parents are committed and practise. There are a variety of pastoral practices in parishes. This is not a debate I wish to take up here, though it has practical and pastoral implications for families, parishes and schools. Each parish and school, within a particular situation, will make decisions on this issue helped by diocesan guidance. Included in discussion of such issues is the question *Who are our schools for?*

Widely varying religious situations

In a previous reflection we noted what the recent Church document had to say about the different types and categories of pupils in our schools, and their different attitudes to faith and religion. Yet, whatever the situations and whatever the difficulties, the text declares that *to these new forms of poverty the Catholic School now turns in a spirit of love*. Pupils in our schools come from a variety of religious experiences and backgrounds. They are at different levels of commitment to Christian beliefs and practices. There are pupils from committed, practising families; many are baptised but have little experience or knowledge of Church and religion. Some are from other Christian traditions, and increasingly in some areas there are pupils from different faiths. It is in a specific context, with pupils and families coming from some of these particular situations, that a Catholic School seeks to help develop the faith and religious development of all pupils.

Various statements address the issue of the faith development of Catholic pupils with different religious back-grounds, experiences and needs. They acknowledge that results or success will vary.

> *Students will surely have many different levels of faith response; the Christian vision of existence must be presented in such a way that it meets all these levels; ranging from the most elementary evangelisation all the way to communion in the same faith. And whatever the situation, the presentation must always be in the nature of gift: though offered insistently and urgently, it cannot be imposed.*[51]

In this context it is useful to reflect on the parable of *The Sower* which depicts a variety of results after the sowing of the seed. This parable was probably told by Jesus to reassure the disciples who were disconcerted, even disillusioned, by the partial success that Jesus himself was having in his ministry and preaching. He touched and cured many, but not all appeared grateful. When invited by him, not all took up the call to follow him. He gathered a small chosen

---

[51]   *Lay Catholics in School: Witnesses to Faith* no 28

band of disciples who struggled and failed, from time to time, to respond to his challenge and follow his way.[52] The parable has much to say to us today. The teacher's attitude and behaviour should be of one preparing the soil.

At times some Catholics maintain that our schools are failing, at least in what is seen as their prime purpose of handing on the faith. One of the documents takes up this issue.

> *Catholic Schools are often accused of not knowing how to form convinced, articulate Christians ready to take their place in social and political life. Every educational enterprise, however, involves the risk of failure and one must not be too discouraged by apparent or even real failures, since there are very many formative influences on young people, and results often have to be calculated on a long-term basis.*[53]

The text discusses the argument put forward by some, that the Church should perhaps give up the mission in Catholic Schools and *direct her energy to more direct work of evangelisation considered to be of higher priority or more suited to her spiritual mission*. The response is clear and forthright:

> *Such a solution would not only be contrary to the directives of the Vatican Council, but would also be opposed to the Church's mission and what is expected of her by Christian people.*[54]

Suitable conditions for faith development

There is much that a school can, and does do, to promote faith development in Catholic and other pupils. In these reflections I can only allude to some aspects of this task. More detailed discussion and guidance will be found in other texts. A passage in the 1971 General Catechetical Directory is helpful. Although the text is addressed to catechists, it clearly has relevance to what chaplains and teachers seek to do in our schools by way of faith, religious and spiritual development of pupils. I quote the passage in full.

---

[52] *Soil for the Seed* Preface
[53] *The Catholic School* no 22
[54] *The Catholic School* no 23

The importance and magnitude of the work to be done by catechists does not prevent the necessary establishing of boundaries around the role of catechists. They are responsible for choosing and creating suitable conditions which are necessary for the Christian message to be sought, accepted, and more profoundly investigated. This is the point to which the action of the catechists extends – and there it stops. For the adherence on the part of those to be taught is the fruit of grace and freedom, and does not ultimately depend on the catechist; and catechetical activity should be accompanied by prayer.[55]

This seems to me an important passage that calls for serious reflection, both on the part of those involved in faith and religious education in our school, and on the part of those who may be critical of the *success* rate of our schools in producing young Catholics who know and practise the faith. For those involved in the task, it may be of some comfort as they walk with the young in their search for meaning and significance in life. For their critics, it is a reminder that while faith is a gift, it is also a free human response of the person. The theologian, now Cardinal, Walter Kasper reminds us,

Faith is a fully and wholly human act in spite of all the indebtedness and bestowal of grace; it is a person who believes and not the Holy Spirit in a person.[56]

There are many influences which affect the life choices of young people and adults and we have to take a more long-term view of how young people are influenced by much of what they experienced in school.

Dimensions of the Christian Faith

A key strand in the Christian ideal of education is the communication of a perspective, centred on faith in Christ as Saviour of all, which discerns a meaning in human life deeper than or beyond the scope of the senses, culture, the pursuit of a career, politics, nationalism, internationalism or any scheme of self-improvement derived solely from human endeavour.

---

[55] *General Directory for Catechesis* no 71
[56] W Kasper *An Introduction to Christian Faith* p 21

While penetrating deeper than these values, it does not deny to any of them their just validity. This perspective is conveyed gradually in ways appropriate to each individual, and its instruments are: explicit religious teaching, the sacramental life, prayer, quiet reflection, example, an appreciation of the works of creation, and especially the growth of human relationships in the light of Christ's commandment of love.[57]

In seeking to choose and create suitable conditions for the faith and religious development of pupils, we could focus on what are described in documents as dimensions; features, characteristics of the Christian faith, which in turn relate to tasks or duties that should be undertaken. First and foremost, faith is *experienced within a community*. This applies to family, parish and school. Within a community, faith is *celebrated, lived* and *prayed*. I wish to reflect briefly on these dimensions or characteristics which relate to activities we can undertake in our schools. We know that not all staff and pupils are of the Catholic faith in our schools. However, I do not believe that reflection on these aspects of faith, and their relation to the actual life of the school will be off-putting to them or seem to ignore or show little respect or concern for them. Sensitively expressed and acted on they encompass all involved in the school and will relate to the religious, spiritual and moral development of pupils. I use the terms of Michael Paul Gallagher which I think speak more immediately and aptly to the school context.[58]

BELONGING

This refers to the sense of welcome, belonging and community that all should experience within the school. Pupils and others can *experience their dignity as persons before they know its definition.* Earlier reflections have focused on this key aspect of the religious dimension of education in our schools which is *not a merely sociological category* but is inspired, motivated and challenged by the belief in Creation and God as Trinity. It refers to the common shared vision and to the healthy and warm relationships among members of staff, pupils and their parents or guardians.

---

[57] *Signposts and Homecomings* pp 119 120
[58] See *Soil for the Seed* pp 202-203

MEANING

This refers to the many opportunities for the exploration of the great questions about life and meaning, of the key human issues that concern the young. Teachers, not only RE teachers, can help pupils consider these in the light of the Christian and other religious beliefs. In this way knowledge *becomes wisdom and life vision* and *the various subjects do not present only knowledge to be attained but also values to be acquired and truths to be discovered.* In this regard reflective assemblies have a key role to play.

LISTENING

This will include opportunities for time and space for quiet, for reflection and prayer, openness to God and others. Well thought-out and reflective assemblies, in which pupils actively participate, are valuable. The provision of a quiet room or chapel available to staff and pupils encourages and enables this reflection. There will be liturgical and extra-liturgical celebrations which meet, in a sensitive way, the different experiences, needs and aspirations of staff and pupils. Experiences offered by *away days*, in the supportive environment of retreat centres, are invaluable for personal and community development. This dimension includes the provision of suitable resources which will help class teachers, and form tutors, facilitate relevant prayerful reflection with their own groups. Attention and respect will be shown to those of other churches and other faiths.

DOING

This looks to the moral and social development of pupils and encourages service, within the school, and in the community beyond the school. Personal issues of particular concern to young people will be seriously considered and discussed. The same will be true also of local and global issues. Pupils should be invited and encouraged to take up work with such agencies as the SVP and CAFOD. Where this is done, not only do the pupils serve the needs of others, but they themselves are enriched in many ways. Again this will be done across the curriculum and not just in religious education lessons. Pupils will be given some voice in running and evaluating certain aspects of school life. In this way they become active agents in their own education and not mere passive recipients of our educational endeavours. This may entail the setting up and the financing of class and school councils.

I present these as some important ways in which our schools can choose and create suitable conditions for the faith, religious and spiritual development of pupils. They are ways in which we can promote faith education, while at the same time respecting freedom of conscience.

Pause for Reflection

In your opinion what are the main negative aspects of today's culture which impact on children and young people?

What are the positive aspects that you find in children and in young people?

In what ways can you acknowledge these?

Can you identify the widely varying religious situations among your pupils?

In what way can and does the school respond to them?

In what ways are sensitivity and respect shown to all, the committed Catholics, those who do not practise, those of other Christian traditions, those of other faiths?

Are you more or less convinced of the value of our Catholic Schools in the light of these reflections?

Can you say why?

Some Final Reflections

The Catholic School, both primary and secondary, is of inestimable value to the life of the Church in England and Wales. Whatever new educational priorities may emerge we must neither belittle the contribution which schools have made in the past, nor underestimate their potential for the future.

The Catholic School should be so inspired by the Gospel that it is seen to be an alternative to other forms of schooling. There are many questions which we need to ask about the Catholic School if it is to fulfil its role as a Gospel inspired community.

Bishops of England and Wales, The Easter People, no 134

The school is undoubtedly a sensitive meeting point for the problems which besiege this restless end of the millennium. This produces a certain degree of pedagogical tiredness, which intensifies the ever increasing difficulty of reconciling the role of the teacher with that of the educator in today's context.

The Catholic School on the Threshold of the Third Millennium no 6

RESOURCES AND REFERENCES

Vatican II Documents
Declaration on Christian Education
Declaration on the Relationship of the Church to non-Christian religions
Pastoral Constitution on the Church in the Modern World.

Papal documents
Paul VI, Evangelisation in the World Today
John Paul II, Catechesis in Our Time
John Paul II, Ecclesia in Europa

Vatican Documents
The Catholic School, Congregation for Catholic Education
Lay Catholics in School – Witnesses to faith, Congregation for Catholic Education
The Religious Dimension of Education in Catholic Schools, Congregation for Catholic Education
General Directory For Catechesis, Congregation for the Clergy
The Catholic School on the Threshold of the New Millennium

All the above documents are available at
http://www.vatican.va/

National Church Documents/Reports
The Easter People, St Paul, 1980
Signposts and Homecomings, St Paul, 1981
Catholic Schools and Children of Other Faiths, Matthew James, 1997
Guidelines for the Study & Implementation of Catholic Schools and Children of Other Faiths. Matthew James, 1997
On The Threshold, Matthew James, 2002

Catholic Education Service Publications

Spiritual and Moral Development Across the Curriculum, 1995
The Common Good in Education, 1997
Evaluating the Distinctive Nature of a Catholic School

Other authors

W Kasper, An Introduction to Faith, Burns & Oates, 1980
M P Gallagher S J, Help My Unbelief, Veritas, 1983
M P Gallagher S J, Free to Believe, DLT, 1987
T Groome, Educating for Life, Thomas More Allen, Texas, 1998
J Gallagher SDB, Soil for the Seed, McCrimmons, 2001